ARACHNID WORLD

JUMPING SPIDERS

SANDRA MARKLE

GOLD-MEDAL STALKERS

⌐ LERNER PUBLICATIONS COMPANY MINNEAPOLIS

FOR CURIOUS KIDS EVERYWHERE

ACKNOWLEDGMENTS

The author would like to thank Dr. Simon Pollard, Canterbury Museum, Christchurch, New Zealand, for sharing his expertise and enthusiasm. A special thanks to Skip Jeffery for his support during the creation of this book.

Lerner Publications Company
A division of Lerner Publishing Group, Inc.
241 First Avenue North
Minneapolis, MN 55401 U.S.A.

Website address: www.lernerbooks.com

Library of Congress Cataloging-in-Publication Data

Markle, Sandra.
    Jumping spiders : gold-medal stalkers / by Sandra Markle.
      p.   cm. — (Arachnid world)
    Includes bibliographical references and index.
    ISBN 978–0–7613–5047–7 (lib. bdg. : alk. paper)
    1. Jumping spiders—Juvenile literature. I. Title.
  QL458.42.S24M33 2012
  595.4'4—dc23   2011021598

Manufactured in the United States of America
1 - DP - 12/31/11

CONTENTS

AN ARACHNID'S WORLD

WELCOME TO THE WORLD OF ARACHNIDS (ah-RACK-nidz). Arachnids can be found in every habitat on Earth except in the deep ocean. Some are even found in Antarctica.

So how can you tell if an animal is an arachnid rather than a relative like an insect *(below)*? Both arachnids and insects belong to a group of animals called arthropods (AR-throh-podz). All the animals in this group share some traits. They have bodies divided into segments, jointed legs, and a stiff exoskeleton. This is a skeleton on the outside like a suit of armor. But one way to tell if an animal is an arachnid is to count its legs and body parts. While not every adult arachnid has eight legs, most do. Arachnids also usually have two main body parts. Most adult insects, like this grasshopper, have six legs and three main body parts.

This book is about jumping spiders, such as this regal jumping spider *(facing page)*. Jumping spiders are gold-medal arachnid stalkers. They can leap as much as forty times their body length to catch prey (living things to eat).

A jumping spider's body temperature rises and falls with the temperature around it. It must warm up to be active.

ON THE OUTSIDE

There are about five thousand different kinds of jumping spiders. They all share certain features. They have two main body parts: the cephalothorax (sef-uh-loh-THOR-ax) and the abdomen. A tiny waistlike bit called the pedicel joins the two. The spider's exoskeleton is made of many plates. Stretchy tissues connect the plates so the spider can bend and move.

Take a close look at this female dimorphic jumping spider to discover other key features these spiders share.

SPINNERETS: These nozzlelike parts spin silk.

LEGS: These are used for walking and climbing. Tiny claws at the tip help the spider grip.

ABDOMEN

CEPHALOTHORAX

EYES:
These organs detect light and send messages to the brain for sight. Jumping spiders have eight eyes.

PEDICEL

PEDIPALPS:
These are a pair of leglike parts that extend from the head near the mouth. They help catch prey and hold it for eating. Males use the pedipalps during mating.

CHELICERAE
(keh-LIH-seh-ree): This pair of jawlike parts is in front of the mouth and ends in fangs. The fangs are used to stab prey and inject venom (liquid poison).

ON THE INSIDE

Look inside an adult female dimorphic jumping spider.

OVARY: This body part produces eggs.

HEART: This muscular tube pumps blood toward the head. Then the blood flows throughout the body and back to the heart.

MALPHIGHIAN (MAHL-pig-ee-an) TUBULES: This system of tubes cleans the blood of wastes.

GUT: This tube lets food nutrients pass into the blood.

STERCORAL (STER-kor-ul) POCKET: The body part where wastes collect before passing out of the body.

SILK GLAND: This body part produces silk.

TRACHEAE (TRAY-kee-ee): These tubes let air enter through holes called spiracles. Tracheae spread oxygen throughout the spider's body.

SPERMATHECA (spur-muh-THEE-kuh): This sac stores sperm after mating.

BOOK LUNGS: These are thin, flat folds of tissue. Oxygen from the air passes through them and enters the spider's blood. Waste carbon dioxide gas exits through them.

SUCKING STOMACH: This stomach works with the pharynx to move food between the mouth and the gut. Cells in the lining produce digestive fluids.

BRAIN: This part sends and receives messages to and from body parts.

Approved by Dr. Simon Pollard, Canterbury Museum, Christchurch, New Zealand

VENOM GLAND: This body part produces venom.

NERVE GANGLIA: These bundles of nerve tissue send messages between the brain and other body parts.

PHARYNX (FAR-inks): This muscular tube moves food into the stomach. Hairs in it help filter out solid waste.

CAECA (SEE-kuh): These branching tubes pass food nutrients into the blood. They also store food.

COXAL (KAHK-sel) GLANDS: These special groups of cells collect liquid wastes and pass them through openings to the outside.

ESOPHAGUS A tube through which food passes on the way to the pharynx.

BECOMING ADULTS

Like all arachnids, jumping spiders go through incomplete metamorphosis (meh-tuh-MOR-fuh-sis). *Metamorphosis* means "change." A jumping spider's life includes three stages: egg, nymph or spiderling, and adult.

Jumping spiders spin silk to protect their eggs. When spiderlings hatch, they are blind and unable to eat. They stay in their silk egg sac until they molt (shed their skin). Then they can see and eat. They chew their way out of the egg sac and go off to live alone. The spiderlings continue to eat and molt to grow bigger until they become adults. At first, when a spiderling molts, its new exoskeleton is soft. The spiderling forces blood into different parts of its body to stretch its soft exoskeleton. This gives it room to grow before it needs to molt again.

Some arthropods go through complete metamorphosis. The stages are egg, larva, pupa, and adult. Each stage looks and behaves very differently.

Compare these canopy jumping spiderlings to their mother. Besides being smaller, spiderlings may be a different color and have different markings. However, they can do anything adults can do except mate and produce young.

CHAMPION HUNTERS

The focus of a jumping spider's life is catching prey to eat. It mainly hunts insects and other arachnids. Lots of other animals are hunting this same prey. But some jumping spiders, like *Euophrys omnisuperstes* (u-OH-feh-ris ahm-neh-SOOP-er-teez), hunt where other spiders won't go. Its scientific name means "standing above everything." It lives high in Asia's Himalayan Mountains, where the weather is some of the fiercest on Earth. This spider has even been found as high as 21,981 feet (6,700 meters) on Mount Everest, the world's highest mountain.

On these craggy mountains, this jumping spider hides in crevices in the rocks. There, it waits to attack the tiny insects that eat bits of plant material blown up from far below.

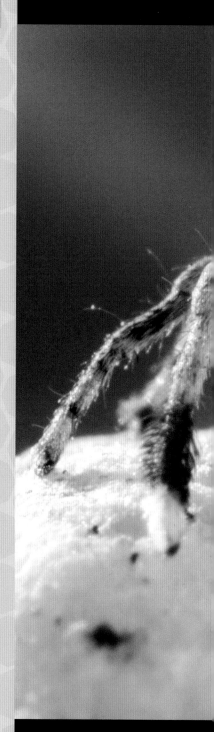

Wherever they live, jumping spiders are equipped to stalk prey. For one thing, most, like *Evarcha arcuata* (ee-VAR-kuh ar-KEW-ah-tuh), which is common throughout Europe, have bodies colored to blend in. This earwig didn't spot the jumping spider until it was too late. The spider snagged its prey.

Even though it's only 0.47 inches (12 millimeters) in size, the female green jumping spider *(below)* is the largest kind of jumping spider in Australia. It's big enough to tackle prey, such as this little frog, that's too big for most spiders. Because this spider blends in, it can stalk its prey without being noticed. It moves closer very slowly, freezing whenever the frog looks its way. That way the spider hides in plain sight. Finally close enough, the spider jumps and sinks in its fangs. This delivers a dose of venom that paralyzes the prey so it can't escape.

The Asian ant-mimic spider has a body shape that is the perfect disguise for hunting weaver ants. This spider adds to its disguise by lifting its front legs and waving them around. This mimics the ants' antennae—body parts spiders don't have.

ANT-MIMIC JUMPING SPIDER

The Panamanian bird-dropping jumping spider is also naturally disguised. Its coloring and shape let it pass for a dab of bird waste dropped on a leaf. When prey, like this fly, lands nearby, the jumping spider slowly slips closer. Anytime the fly looks its way, the spider freezes. Then it creeps forward again until it's close enough to jump and bite.

Of course, having a good disguise is only part of being a successful stalker. Jumping spiders have especially sharp vision to watch for their prey. Jumping spiders have eight eyes: four looking forward, two on top of their head, and two toward the back of their cephalothorax. Having eyes aimed in so many different directions gives the jumping spider a very broad field of view. That's how this magnolia green jumping spider caught the fly. The two large middle eyes are thought to have among the sharpest vision of any arachnid. Jumping spiders are known to spot prey as much as twenty body lengths—up to 15 inches (38 centimeters)—away. The spider can also look left, right, up, and down with its big eyes. But the spider's eyes don't move the way human eyes move. Each eye is inside a tube, like looking through a telescope. When the spider looks in one direction and then another, its whole eye tube moves.

JUMPING SPIDER FACT

When the eye of a jumping spider looks dark, the angle is straight down the eye tube to the retina. The retina is a layer of light-sensitive cells that sends signals to the brain. When the spider's eye tube is looking in another direction, the eye appears partly light.

Jumping spiders can move their big middle eyes independently. So they can look in different directions at once.

Some jumping spiders, like this Australian fringed jumping spider, use tricks to catch prey. When the fringed spider discovers another spider hiding inside a rolled-up leaf, it slowly and carefully climbs onto the leaf. Then it taps its legs on the leaf. Sensing small movements that could mean prey walking on its leaf, the other spider rushes out of hiding ready to attack. But the bigger fringed jumping spider is waiting. The fringed jumping spider usually walks slowly with jerky movements. But the spider is capable of bursting into action when it leaps. Its prey can't escape fast enough so the fringed jumping spider catches its meal.

The fringed jumping spider also uses a trick to snatch spiders that spin webs to catch flying prey. The fringed jumping spider grabs some of the web strands with its hook-tipped feet *(below)*. Then it plucks those strands in a pattern it repeats over and over. It varies the tugs until it gets a response. Hiding nearby while holding onto strands of its web, the web-building spider senses these movements. They may seem to signal trapped prey. Or the movments might trick a female web builder into thinking a male is signaling it's coming to mate. Whatever the trick, the fringed jumping spider fools the other spider. When it's close enough, the fringed jumping spider pounces and bites its prey.

Of course, what makes jumping spiders champion stalkers is that they can catch prey across a distance. When the golden jumping spider spots a cricket, the spider follows it with its big middle eyes. At the same time, the spider produces silk and uses its feet to attach a silk pad to the leaf it's on. Next, the jumping spider creeps forward slowly. As it moves, it produces more silk, playing out this safety line behind itself. The cricket stops. The jumping spider stops too. Its eyes are locked onto its potential prey, its body is lowered, and its legs are bent. The spider is ready to jump.

Suddenly, muscles inside the spider's body contract, forcing blood into its four hind legs. This causes them to quickly stretch out and launch the spider forward. As the spider flies through the air, it continually produces silk, stretching out its safety line. This keeps the spider from crashing if it falls. But it doesn't fall. It lands on the cricket. ZAP! The spider bites to kill.

LEAPING FOR A LIVING

It's a sunny summer day in Ohio when this female *Phiddipus clarus* (FIHD-eh-puhs KLAIR-uhs) goes hunting. Like most jumping spiders, she hunts during the day to make the most of her excellent eyesight. She climbs easily, even on slick plant stems. Unlike spiders that spend their lives on their webs, she has more than claws on the tips of her feet. Each foot ends in a tuft of special hairs. Like suction cups, these hairs help her grip most surfaces.

FOOT

Wherever she travels, the female jumping spider trails a silk safety line. From time to time, she produces a bit of sticky silk to glue this line to the surface she's crossing. So when she jumps to leap between two leaves and misses, she doesn't fall far. She uses the two claws on each foot to grip the line, turn around, and climb back up. Then she crawls on, searching for prey.

JUMPING SPIDER FACT

Jumping spiders can even climb glass. That's because the tuft of hair on their feet tips can grip the tiny bumps—the imperfections—on the surface of the glass.

SAFETY LINE

When she sits still, the female *Phiddipus clarus* looks like a bit of debris (garbage) on a leaf and hides in plain sight. She waits and watches. When no prey appears, she moves on and then sits still to hide again. Finally, she spots a deer fly. Her eyes lock on the fly as it swoops and circles.

As the deer fly wings past, the female jumping spider leaps. This time she grabs her prey and bites. Her bite injects the dose of venom that paralyzes the prey. She bites again, injecting some digestive juices with her venom *(facing page)*. Then she holds onto her prey and waits. The digestive juices turn the prey's soft tissue into a kind of liquid power drink. Next, the muscles around her stomach relax, creating a sucking force. This pulls the liquid food out of the prey's exoskeleton and into the jumping spider's body.

The spider injects more digestive juices and repeats the process. Finally, only the prey's empty exoskeleton remains. The spider drops this garbage.

JUMPING SPIDER FACT

Scientific tests have shown jumping spiders can see colors. They are also able to detect ultraviolet (UV) light human eyes can't see.

The female jumping spider eats and grows bigger. Before long, she is too big for her exoskeleton. It is time to molt again. She has already molted five times before. She spins silk threads and attaches them to a leaf. Then she grips these with her feet. Her exoskeleton splits open. When the female pulls her body out of the old skin, she is an adult.

MOLTED SKIN

This was her final molt. She's an adult ready to reproduce. She keeps on hunting and eating. But this time, her energy goes into producing eggs. To help *Phiddipus clarus* males find her, she coats her safety line with pheromones (FAIR-uh-mohnz). Pheromones are chemical signals. They tell the male *Phiddipus clarus* that the female is ready to mate.

JUMPING SPIDER FACT

Phiddipus clarus males will only mate with *Phiddipus clarus* females.

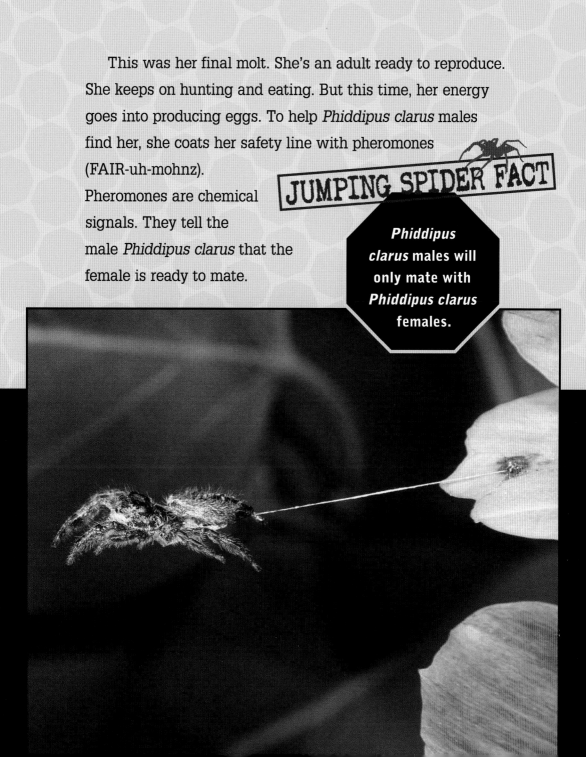

FINDING A MATE

As in most jumping spiders, a mature male *Phiddipus clarus*
(below) does not look like the female. For one thing, he has
much bigger chelicerae. He'll need these and strength to
win a mate. More than one male is likely to follow a female's
pheromone trail. Then the males fight each other. They do this

by shaking their abdomen really quickly and waving their legs. Once they are close enough, one will push the other. This goes on until one gives up. That loser leaves to search for another female. The winner shakes his abdomen superfast as a sign of his victory. Then he gets ready to attract the female.

Before he starts, the male *Phiddipus clarus* spins a tiny web. He crawls over this and deposits his sperm (male reproductive cells) on it. He picks up the sperm with one of his pedipalps. Then he goes after the female, carrying his sperm packet.

JUMPING SPIDER FACT

Male jumping spiders often mature a couple of weeks faster than females. One lucky enough to find an immature female will guard her until she is ready to mate.

SPERM PACKET

When the male jumping spider gets within sight of the female, he pauses. He weaves back and forth and waves his pedipalps. He also taps his feet *(below)*, his abdomen, and his cephalothorax on the surface. He repeats these actions over and over.

The female jumping spider can see him clearly. She watches his every move *(below)*. Although human ears can't hear any sound, her sensitive hairs pick up the movements he's making. She recognizes him as a *Phiddipus clarus* male ready to mate. So she does not attack as he moves closer.

The male finally reaches the female. He inserts his sperm into her gonopore (reproductive opening). The sperm will be stored in the spermatheca, a special sac, until she's ready to deposit her eggs.

The male jumping spider leaves. He may hunt for another female and repeat the mating process. But he won't live much longer.

FEMALE

MALE

The female goes hunting again. She needs to catch and eat more prey. This food gives her the energy she needs for her eggs to fully develop.

THE CYCLE CONTINUES

Next, the female finds a sheltered spot. There she spins a tentlike silk pouch. This will provide protection from the weather and help shield her from other hungry hunters.

Inside the tent, she spins a silk disk. She deposits her eggs one at a time on this disk. As each egg cell leaves her body through her gonopore, it passes the male's sperm stored in the spermatheca. When egg and sperm join, a baby spider starts to develop. A tough coating forms around the egg cell. As soon she finishes laying her eggs—nearly one hundred in all—she'll spin more silk to form an egg sac around them.

The female stands guard over her eggs, fighting off any hunters. She stays on duty for about a month until the young hatch. Then she leaves. She needs to hunt again, catch more prey, and get the energy to lay another mass of eggs. She will be able to produce eggs as many as six more times without mating again. Once they hatch, the spiderlings *(below)* quickly leave the egg sac and begin to hunt to feed themselves.

JUMPING SPIDER FACT

During the summer months, each egg sac the female produces contains fewer eggs than the one before.

Some spiderlings are eaten by other hunters—even other *Phiddipus clarus*. Those that survive grow bigger. Those able to catch more prey grow bigger faster than others. But by the time cold autumn winds are tearing the last leaves from tree branches, many jumping spiderlings are nearly adult size. All the young spiders spin tentlike webs as shelters where they can rest over the winter. Their father died long ago. Their mother dies soon after they move into their shelters. In the spring, when prey is plentiful again, young spiders will leave their shelters and go hunting. Then they'll become adults, mate, and the jumping spider life cycle will continue.

JUMPING SPIDERS AND OTHER STALKING ARACHNIDS

JUMPING SPIDERS BELONG TO A GROUP, or order, of arachnids called Araneae (ah-RAN-ee-ay). These are the spider members of the arachnid group. Jumping spider is the common name for spiders that belong to a family of spiders called the Salticidae (sahl-TIHS-ee-dee). There are about five thousand different kinds worldwide. This is the largest family of spiders.

SCIENTISTS GROUP living and extinct animals with others that are similar. So jumping spiders are classified this way:

kingdom: Animalia
phylum: Arthropoda
class: Arachnida
order: Araneae
family: Salticidae

HELPFUL OR HARMFUL? Jumping spiders are both, but they're mainly helpful because they eat a lot of insects. This helps control insect populations that could otherwise become pests. They may be harmful because, while they only bite in self-defense, their bite does inject venom. Jumping spider venom usually doesn't hurt people. Some people though may have an allergic reaction to a spider's bite.

HOW BIG IS a *Phiddipus clarus*? A female's body is 0.39 inches (10 mm) long.

MORE STALKING ARACHNIDS

Jumping spiders are gold-medal stalkers, but other arachnids are successful stalkers too. Compare the way these arachnids hunt.

Lone star ticks are a North American arachnid found especially in the southern and eastern parts of the United States. This tick is equipped with special sensors to stalk its prey. Like all ticks, a lone star tick needs a blood meal to survive and continue its life cycle. Unlike most ticks that sit and wait to ambush a host, a lone star tick wanders in search of a host. When its senses one, it moves closer. The tick may even move quickly for a short distance to reach the host before it can escape.

Spitting spiders are a kind of spider found worldwide that can attack from a distance. Being tiny—just 0.2 inches (6 mm) long—the spitting spider can slip unnoticed near resting mosquitoes or flies. Then the spider squeezes two glands in its cephalothorax. This action forces gummy threads out a hole at the tip of each of its fangs. At the same time, it sways from side to side. This causes the liquid to zigzag across the prey's back and onto the surrounding surface. The liquid dries almost instantly, trapping the prey. Because the liquid holds venom, the prey quickly becomes paralyzed. Once its prey is trapped this way, the little spider quickly moves in to make the kill.

GLOSSARY

abdomen: the rear end of an arachnid. It contains systems for digestion, reproduction and, in spiders, silk production.

adult: the reproductive stage of an arachnid's life cycle

book lungs: thin flat folds of tissue where blood circulates. Air enters through slits and passes between these tissue folds, allowing oxygen to enter the blood. Waste carbon dioxide gas exits through them.

brain: this organ receives messages from the rest of the body and sends signals to control all body parts

caeca: branching tubes through which liquid food passes and where food is stored

cephalothorax: the front end of an arachnid. It includes the mouth, the brain, and the eyes. Legs are also attached to this part.

chelicerae: a pair of strong, jawlike parts that extend from the head in front of the mouth and end in fangs to inject venom

coxal glands: special groups of cells for collecting and getting rid of liquid wastes through openings to the outside of the body. They aid in maintaining water balance in the body.

debris: bits of waste or garbage

egg: a female reproductive cell; also the name given to the first stage of an arachnid's life cycle

exoskeleton: a protective, armorlike covering on the outside of the body

eyes: sensory organs that detect light and send signals to the brain for sight

fang: one of a pair of toothlike parts of the spider's chelicerae. Venom flows out of the fang through a hole near the tip.

gonopore: the female reproductive opening

gut: the body part through which food nutrients pass into the blood and are carried throughout the body

heart: the muscular tube that pumps blood throughout the body and back to the heart

Malpighian tubules: a system of tubes that cleans the blood of wastes and dumps them into the intestine

molt: to shed the exoskeleton

nerve ganglia: bundles of nerve tissue that send messages between the brain and other body parts

ovary: the body part that produces eggs

pedicel: the waistlike part in spiders that connects the cephalothorax to the abdomen

pedipalps: a pair of leglike body parts that extend from the head near the mouth. They help catch prey and hold it for eating. In males the pedipalps are also used during reproduction.

pharynx: a muscular body part that contracts to create a pumping force, drawing food into the body's digestive system

pheromones: chemicals given off as a form of communication

safety line: a silk line a spider spins and anchors to the surface it crosses

silk gland: the body part that produces silk

sperm: a male reproductive cell

spermatheca: the sac in female arachnids where sperm is stored after mating

spiderling: the stage between egg and adult in spiders

spinneret: the body part that spins silk

spiracle: a small opening in the exoskeleton that leads into the tracheae

stercoral pocket: a place where wastes collect before passing out of the body

sucking stomach: a muscular body part that works with the pharynx to pull liquid food into the arachnid's gut

tracheae: tubes through which air enters via openings, called spiracles. The tubes help spread and store oxygen throughout the spider's body.

venom: liquid poison

venom gland: the body part that produces venom

DIGGING DEEPER

To keep on investigating jumping spiders, explore these books and online sites.

BOOKS

Bishop, Nic. *Nic Bishop Spiders*. New York: Scholastic, 2007. Wonderful color photos bring facts to life. Compare jumping spiders to the other spiders presented in this book.

Markle, Sandra. *Sneaky Spinning Baby Spiders*. New York: Walker Books for Young Readers, 2008. Compare the way jumping spiderlings hatch and grow up to the life cycles of other kinds of spiders.

McGinty, Alice B. *The Jumping Spider*. New York: PowerKids Press, 2005. Take an additional look at jumping spiders hunting in their natural habitat.

Singer, Marilyn. *Venom*. Minneapolis: Millbrook Press, 2007. Learn about the creatures that can harm or kill with a bite or a sting.

Souza, D. M. *Packed with Poison!* Minneapolis: Millbrook Press, 2006. Read about the most venomous and poisonous animals in the world.

MORE FROM SANDRA MARKLE

ARACHNID WORLD:
Black Widows
Harvestmen
Orb Weavers
Scorpions
Ticks
Wolf Spiders

WEBSITES

Jumping Spiders

http://www.xs4all.nl/~ednieuw/Spiders/Salticidae/Salticidae.htm
This site has wonderful photos of jumping spiders to enjoy. There are also fascinating facts to discover.

Bee vs. Jumping Spider

http://www.youtube.com/watch?v=qxbuysNGLOM
Watch a jumping spider catch a bee. Check out the roll its big and small eyes play in the attack. Don't miss the silk safety line the spider uses to stay safe when it leaps.

Kentucky Spiders:
Jumping Spiders

http://www.uky.edu/Ag/
CritterFiles/casefile/spiders/
jumping/jumping.htm
Explore interesting facts and great photos showing the lives and behavior of jumping spiders. Follow links to investigate jumping spiders from different parts of the world.

LERNER   SOURCE™

Visit www.lerneresource.com **for free, downloadable arachnid diagrams, research assignments to use with this series, and additional information about arachnid scientific names.**

JUMPING SPIDER ACTIVITY

Jumping spiders can jump at least two to three times their body length. Some can leap as much as forty times their body length. How does your jumping ability compare?

Have an adult partner measure how tall you are. Your height is your body length. Then work with your adult partner to find a place that will be safe for you to jump, such as onto tumbling mats or an air mattress. Mark a starting line. You'll need to start your jump from standing at that line. Jumping spiders leap from the point where they stop stalking their prey.

When you're ready, jump. Then use a measuring tape to find out how far away you landed. Were you able to jump as far as twice your body length?

Here's another way to understand the jumping spider's ability. Multiply your body length by forty. Now go outdoors and measure off that distance from a starting point. Imagine being able to jump that far in a single leap—as far as a jumping spider sometimes jumps!

INDEX

PHOTO ACKNOWLEDGMENTS

The images in this book are used with the permission of: © NHPA/SuperStock, p. 4; © James Carmichael Jr./NHPA/Photoshot, pp. 4–5, 11, 17, 18–19, 36; © George Grall/ National Geographic/Getty Images, pp. 6–7; © Laura Westlund/Independent Picture Service, pp. 8–9; © Gavin Maxwell/naturepl.com, pp. 12–13; © Stephen Dalton/naturepl.com, p. 14; © Minden Pictures/SuperStock, pp. 15, 16, 20, 21, 41 (bottom); © Martin Dohrn/Photo Researchers, Inc., pp. 22–23; © Susumu Nishinaga/Photo Researchers, Inc., p. 24; © Dwight Kuhn, pp. 24–25, 27, 28, 29, 30, 31, 35, 37, 38; © Joe Warfel/Eighth-Eye Photography, pp. 32, 33, 34, 39; Centers for Disease Control and Prevention Public Health Image Library/James Gathany, p. 41 (top); © Kim Taylor/naturepl.com, pp. 46–47.

Front cover: © Simon Pollard.

Main body text set in Glypha LT Std 55 Roman 12/20. Typeface provided by Adobe Systems.